SALT and LIGHT
POCKET GUIDES

COMING TO GRIPS WITH
SATAN'S PLAN
FOR YOUR LIFE

COMING TO GRIPS WITH SATAN'S PLAN FOR YOUR LIFE

ERWIN W. LUTZER

MOODY PRESS

CHICAGO

© 1990 by
ERWIN W. LUTZER

ISBN: 0-8024-3544-0

3 4 5 6 Printing/VP/Year 94 93 92 91

Printed in the United States of America

Coming to Grips with
Satan's Plan for Your Life

"God loves you and has a wonderful plan for your life!"

That's the good news.

The bad news is that Satan hates you and has a *destructive* plan for your life.

Even secularists are beginning to believe. Newspapers carry stories of demon worship and openly discuss the growing belief that there is a personal devil. We should not be surprised that there is empirical evidence that Satan exists, for we have met him in our own lives and in the experiences of others. More important, we know incredible details about him from the pages of the Bible. Not only does he exist, but he is actively seeking recruits.

In fact, I believe that *he has already made meticulous plans for our downfall.* All that is left for us to do is to step into the carefully laid trap. Unfortunately, the trap is hidden—it blends in with our aptitudes and surroundings and looks as if it is the route to fulfillment. Though it appears harmless, the consequences could be disastrous should we fall into it.

Satan is on the prowl, stalking and setting traps for God's people (and yes, for unbelievers, too). He stays out of view, waiting for an unguarded moment. If we could know the extent of his knowledge of us . . . if we could understand his fiendish delight should we become a discredit to Christ, we would pore over the Scriptures to learn about him and about the weaponry God has given us for the battle.

Satan himself is abhorrent to us. Knowing that, he comes using different disguises and different names. His goal is *to get us to do something he wants while making us think that the idea is wholly ours.*

Understandably, his chief point of attack is the human mind. He has varying degrees of access (depending on the amount of sin we tolerate) and uses his opportunities to the hilt. Since he is not a gentleman and plays only by his own rules, he influences our thoughts and feelings without formal invitation. He is most pleased when his activity is completely hidden.

To alleviate any suspicion or fear, he gives his ideas familiar names that make us feel comfortable. Even the wolf in Little Red Riding Hood was cunning enough to know that he could not say to the grandmother, "Let me in, for I am the wolf!" Instead he disguised his voice and whispered, "I'm Little Red Riding Hood!"

Satan's full-time occupation is *making sin look good to us*. Whatever the lure he employs, it is a highly intelligent spiritual being who plots our downfall. His intention is to cause us shame and to neutralize our effectiveness for Christ.

Satan also has tens of thousands of lesser spirits under his authority who have varying degrees of intelligence and power. They are highly organized and are forced to become his mercenaries, his servants who do his bidding. If they disobey, they are likely punished by their cruel leader.

Of course there would still be addictions, violence, and wasted lives in the world if Satan and his demons did not exist. We have a sin nature that is capable of every kind of evil. Satan, however, plays a key role in tempting us, and, should we say yes to his promptings, he will tighten the chains to keep us bound.

And now for his plan for our lives.

Hunters study animals to become familiar with their likes and dislikes, their habits and whereabouts. Animals don't usually get caught by accident; they are lured into circumstances that look attractive but conceal a deadly hook. If you are catching a mouse you use cheese; a bear will be drawn to a piece of fresh meat; for fish you use worms. You promise your prey what it wants to have but give it what you want it to have. Let's apply this simple analogy to satanic entrapment.

First, Satan tries to develop a keen understanding of his intended victim. Just as we know that mice prefer cheese to dead worms, so Satan knows our weaknesses and habits. He and his demons are keen observers of human nature, but he needs even more specific knowledge of each victim in order to set a trap that will succeed. It is reasonable to assume that evil spirits (one or more) are actually assigned to us to observe our habits and weaknesses.

Second, just as we must determine whether the mouse lives in the basement or the bedroom, so evil spirits observe where we work and with whom we work. They are particularly interested in our daily habits. Of even greater interest is our secret life—those attitudes and behaviors that we keep from others. This provides them with perhaps the most fruitful area of temptation.

Third, just as it would be foolish for us to think we could catch a mouse without a trap, so Satan knows that he must remain hidden. A mousetrap is important because it can be used in our stead; it can catch our victim while we remain out of view. Furthermore, a trap can hold out the promise of food and fulfillment while keeping the ultimate consequences concealed. Mice see only the cheese and do not understand the wire and the powerful spring. Likewise, Satan wants to keep us ignorant of the intriguing dynamics taking place in the spirit world. He wants our circumstances to appear to be ordinary; his traps do not arouse undue suspicion. Yet *behind the trap is the trapper; behind the lie is the liar.*

Satan has as many lures as there are human weaknesses. To change the analogy, he leads us into a hallway with many different doors. To him it does not matter which of these doors we choose, because any one of them will lead to the same dark room of satanic involvement and control.

Later in this booklet, I will list twelve of the most common doors that unsuspecting humans enter. But here I simply point out that Satan exploits our weaknesses; his strategy is for us to fulfill some secret passion, some aspiration of the flesh, some kind of occult practice or rebellion. We are free to choose as we wish. Any one of a hundred doors will do.

Satan's greatest desire is to dethrone God and put himself in charge of the universe. That is impossible, of course, and he knows it. So he must settle for a lesser objective, namely to frustrate the plan of God. This he cannot do. Nevertheless he continues to plunge blindly toward actions that increase his own torment.

His strategy is twofold: (1) make sure that unbelievers are comfortable with their unbelief, blinding the minds of those who do not believe (2 Corinthians 4:3-4), and (2) destroy our effectiveness as Christians by gaining a measure of control in our lives (1 Timothy 4:1-3).

Several levels of control exist, which are not always clearly distinguishable but nevertheless provide a general understanding of the extent of demonization in the lives of people.

STAGE 1

As we have learned, Satan begins by injecting into our minds thoughts that we think are our own. This enables him to remain hidden while luring us into sin. This is brilliant strategy because although sin is attractive to believers, Satan is not. If he were to appear to us, we would be terrified; but because we think these thoughts are wholly ours, we have no fear.

Second, this enables him to work through our existing weaknesses. He takes the sins of the flesh and strengthens their power. By making sin attractive he reinforces the evil that already exists in the human heart. In this way he can capitalize on our weaknesses without arousing suspicion and fear.

If we welcome these thoughts into our minds and if they find a home in our hearts, Satan moves to the second level.

STAGE 2

Satan now takes another step in his quest to control humans. The individual now has given him a stronghold: a deeply rooted tendency to repeat sinful, destructive behavior. Some people are preoccupied with covetousness, moral impurity, rebellion, bitterness, or anger. Although the individual may be freed from these sins for periods of time, he or she will fall back into the same rut when the conditions are right.

Thus Satan disguises himself with the sins of the flesh, magnifying their strength and attractiveness.

STAGE 3

Some people experience obsession, which may be a sign of actual demonic invasion. In these cases the victim is not only preoccupied with these thoughts and behaviors but is controlled by them. The obsessive power of evil occupies his mind at almost every waking moment.

At this level there may be such outward signs as compulsive behavior, uncontrolled passion for various drugs, sexual promiscuity, and eating disorders. In others one may see the desire for revenge, indescribable hostility, or irrational behavior. These people may desire to make progress in the Christian life but find that this barrier is always present. Even when there appears to be some progress, the obsession continues to rear its ugly head from time to time.

Again let me stress that many of the symptoms listed above may exist without demonic activity. Satan simply makes the behavioral ruts deeper so that change becomes more difficult.

At this stage the demonic spirits reinforce their control in the human body. The individual often becomes passive; he is so engulfed by evil that a spirit seems to have complete control over him. In extreme instances he may be overcome by supernatural physical strength and find that his vocal cords are controlled by alien powers. There can be withdrawal, compulsiveness, and self-inflicted torture (see Mark 5).

Christians can usually successfully fight levels 1 and 2 on their own. If they repent of all known sin, obey God's Word, put on the armor of God, and fill their lives with music that praises God, these practices will restrict the enemy's powers.

However, levels 3 and 4 almost always necessitate help from other believers. Jesus taught that some spirits do not go away except by prayer and fasting.

Theologians debate whether demonic spirits can actually inhabit a Christian. Since the New Testament uses the word *demonization* for those who are afflicted by the devil, we can understand that there may be different levels of control and effects. It is not always easy to discern whether a demonic spirit is actually within the person or whether he is doing his work from the outside.

The extent to which a believer can be demonized involves a lengthy discussion beyond the scope of this booklet. Let it simply be said that Christians who have been invaded by demonic spirits prior to their conversion often give evidence that all the spirits do not leave after conversion. Also those who are involved in perpetual disobedience may find that a spirit attaches itself to their personalities. There is ample evidence that Christians can and do experience stages 1 through 3 as outlined above. For further study I recommend *Demon Possession and the Christian—A New Perspective,* by C. Fred Dickason (Crossway, 1989).

To better understand the reason for Satan's anger and the goals he seeks to accomplish, we must now paint the big picture. What was the motive behind his rebellion against God? On what basis can we know he is defeated? What are those doors that we can unwittingly open that will give him a measure of control in our lives? And finally, what can we do to protect ourselves against him and to help those who are bound by him?

What is this conflict all about?

Thanks to Milton's *Paradise Lost* most of us were taught to believe that Lucifer (later called Satan) had his original abode in heaven and was cast out because of his rebellion. It is more likely, however, that Lucifer was ruling the world long before his fall.

Two expressions in Ezekiel 28 give us a hint about his duties. "You were the anointed cherub who covers, and I placed you there. You were on the holy mountain of God; you walked in the midst of the stones of fire" (v. 14).

The phrase "anointed cherub" refers to some kind of priesthood exercised before his fall. This is further confirmed by the reference to "sanctuaries" (v. 18). Possibly he was the guardian cherub, the chief of the honor guard.

The second phrase, "the mountain of God," symbolizes the rule that Lucifer was given, most likely over the whole world.

Putting those two phrases together, we may conclude that Lucifer was given the responsibility of ruling the world by making sure that the worship of all other angelic beings honored God. As Barnhouse wrote in *The Invisible War*, "It would appear that he received the worship of the universe beneath him and offered it to the Creator above him" (Zondervan, 1965).

At that time there was but one ruling will in the universe. God's honor prevailed in the actions and thoughts of all of His creation. There was harmony, fulfillment, and holiness.

Then follows one of the most probing passages in all the Bible. "You were blameless in your ways from the day you were created, until unrighteousness was found in you" (v. 15). The text continues, "By the abundance of your trade you were internally filled with violence, and you sinned" (v. 16).

Sin began in the heart of Lucifer; it came about that in his transactions with God ("the abundance of your trade") he became dishonest. *He began to take that which belonged to God and keep it for himself.* Thus his heart was filled with violence and rebellion.

That was the beginning of the conflict of the ages, the conflict between the will of God and the will of His creatures, between good and evil, between light and darkness, between Creator and creature.

Satan could not have foreseen the consequences of his action, since there had been no other example of rebellion in the universe. Unfortunately, he had to learn the devastation of sin by experience. In retrospect he might have regretted what he had done, but it was too late.

Once the battle lines were drawn and Satan was forced to entrench himself against God, he became wholly evil. He was not on a par with the Almighty, so there was little use pressing for a truce. Nor could he retreat, for evil can never be satisfied with a humble admission of defeat. Having chosen his path, Satan was compelled to follow his evil nature to its destructive end. Never again would he return to his original position. Indeed, he could not even if he had willed to do so.

With the stage set for the conflict, several conclusions immediately emerged.

First, Satan's right to rule the world was not revoked as a result of his sin. Satan promised Christ the kingdoms of the world in exchange for worship and then added, "For it has been handed over to me, and I give it to whomever I wish" (Luke 4:6). Because Satan is a deceiver, some Bible scholars have disputed his grandiose claim that he had been handed the kingdoms of the world. But it is unlikely that Satan would lie to Christ in the same way that he lies to us. He originally was given dominion over the earth, and he still retains it today.

Second, in contrast to God, whose nature is based on truth, Satan became the embodiment of deception. His entire kingdom is based on lies. Jesus said to the Pharisees, "You are of your father the devil, and you want to do the desires of your father. He was a murderer from the beginning, and does not stand in the truth, because there is no truth in him. Whenever he speaks a lie, he speaks from his own nature; for he is a liar, and the father of lies" (John 8:44). It has been aptly said that the only time we can believe the devil is when he tells us he is lying!

"There is no truth in him." What a revealing commentary on Satan's strategy! When we see him operating in the world, the watchword is deception. Since he is devoid of moral principles and sympathy, no atrocity can be considered too evil, no suffering too painful, and no treachery too vile. He employs *any* evil deception to achieve his ends.

Third, Satan is angry. His hatred toward God is irrational and intense. Irrational, because his predicament was brought on by his own rebellion; intense, because he knows that his time is short. Regardless of how many years he has left, he must face the awful reality that eventually he will be thrown into hell forever. The fact that he has already been check-mated and forced to admit defeat fuels his anger. His primary target is the people of God, for *he attacks us in a vain attempt to get back at God.*

Fourth, evidence exists that a multitude of angels fell with Satan and now serve him in forced obedience. The devil himself is not omni-present. Though he can travel quickly, he can only be in one place at a time. Yet, through his mercenaries, who are organized according to rank and responsibility, he can appear to be present everywhere at the same time.

Fifth, Satan will not and cannot be redeemed. His transformation into a throughly evil being is so complete that he would never desire reconciliation with God. But even if he did, God could not allow such an act.

Scripture requires that a redeemer take on the nature of the one being redeemed. Thus Christ had to become man in order to redeem mankind. "For assuredly He does not give help to angels, but He gives help to the descendant of Abraham. Therefore, He had to be made like His brethren in all things, that He might become a merciful and faithful high priest in things pertaining to God, to make propitiation [reconciliation] for the sins of the people" (Hebrews

2:16-17). Christ's sacrifice on the cross can be only applied to the human race; it cannot benefit fallen angels.

Satan's rebellion is the greatest mistake any creature has ever made. Knowing that it can never be undone only adds to his misery and anger. His foolish plan of self-exaltation backfired, forcing him to endure an eternity of suffering and defeat.

But fallen angels are not the only ones in rebellion against God. The human race is also involved in the continuing conflict.

His Greatest Deception

God could have exterminated Satan or confined him to another planet. But He chose instead to let him rule the world and to allow evil to take its destructive course. In the end, God's plan will triumph on the earth, but it will be through conflict, not by sovereign fiat.

Thus after the creation of Adam and Eve, Satan appeared in the Garden of Eden to lure our first parents away from obeying God. Please note carefully: by that point Satan was keenly aware that his act of disobedience had transformed him into a wicked being, the moral antithesis of God.

He was irritated by the fellowship that existed between man and

God. No doubt it reminded him of the time when he had experienced such a blessed relationship. Not content with his own evil nature or any comradery with other fallen angels, he sought to draw mankind into his misery. This appeared to be a master stroke against God.

Let us examine Satan's deceptive ploy at work.

First, he cast doubt on the integrity of God. "Indeed, has God said, 'You shall not eat from any tree of the garden?'" (Genesis 3:1). Whether we accept the translation of the King James Version, *"every* tree of the garden,"* or the *New American Standard Version*, *"any* tree of the garden,"* (italics mine), the point is the same: "Do you mean to tell me that God has restricted you—for no good reason?"

The strategy was brilliant. By asking a question, he avoided directly attacking God, which would have aroused suspicion. Yet he had introduced the thought that perhaps God's command was arbitrary and unnecessary. He had opened the door for "rational" dialogue.

Note how his question got Eve to shift her focus: rather than focusing on the hundreds of trees from which she could eat, she began to concentrate on the one tree that was forbidden.

Second, he contradicted God directly. If Eve ate of the forbidden fruit, he claimed that she would not die but would become "like God, knowing good and evil" (v. 5). That was a direct attack on the motive of God. The command, Satan says, was not for Eve's benefit but to protect God's selfish interests. The Almighty fears rivalry in His kingdom, he insinuated. He is intimidated by all that Eve will become if she eats the fruit. If God really loved Eve He would let her eat, but because of His own selfish interests He makes a restriction. What kind of a God would do that?

When Satan saw both Adam and Eve eat the forbidden fruit, he must have had a moment of fiendish delight. The human race had joined his rebellion. He had tricked these two foolish people into defying the Almighty.

And so a drop of Satan's rebellion now falls on every human heart. Not only is every child born under the legal condemnation of Adam's sin, but each has a sin nature that exerts self-will rather than the will of God. Satan assumed that the whole human race would become as wicked and irredeemable as he.

But that was not to be.

Satan is not omniscient; his knowledge is limited. He can only predict the future based on past observations. Perhaps you have wondered whether or not a fortune-teller (assuming that he or she is under the power of Satan) is able to predict the future. The answer is no. Satan cannot know the future with accuracy. In the Old Testament the mark of a false prophet was that his predictions would sometimes be wide of the mark.

After President Kennedy was shot in 1963, several soothsayers came forward to claim that they had predicted the assassination. How much foreknowledge can Satan have of such events? He can know that a man is planning to shoot the president (indeed he may plant the idea in the assassin's mind), but *he cannot be sure that the assassination will be accomplished as planned.* For all Satan knows, the perpetrator may be arrested for carrying a gun into the Dallas Book Room Depository Building, or the bullet might miss the president, or the gun may jam. In other words, Satan can only know what is being planned; he cannot know for certain whether the plans will fail or succeed. His observation of human nature and his past experience do give him a relatively good idea of what lies ahead, but too many variables exist outside the realm of his control.

If Satan cannot foreknow human events, he obviously could not have foreseen that God would create a plan to redeem fallen humanity. He had to stand by helplessly as God selected some members of the human race to be redeemed and to receive privileges greater than those of angels. They were actually given positions of honor, such as heirs of God and joint-heirs of Christ.

In the Garden of Eden, with the first flush of guilt embedded in Adam and Eve's consciences, God gave them a promise in the form of a judgment on Satan. "And I will put enmity between you and the woman, and between your seed and her seed; He shall bruise you on the head, and you shall bruise him on the heel" (Genesis 3:15).

That was a promise of redemption for our first parents. Though there would be conflict throughout the ages, the seed of the woman would crush the head of the serpent. The serpent would retaliate by bruising the heel of the woman's seed.

What a cruel surprise for Satan! How he hates those human beings whom God so mercifully exalts.

THE GREATEST DEFEAT

For several thousand years the conflict progressed. Satan was permitted to score notable victories. The ancient worlds of Babylon, Greece, and Rome were steeped in occult religions, indirectly giving allegiance to the prince of darkness. There was immorality, cruelty, and numerous false religions. More important, knowledge of the true God was scarcely found on the earth.

But centuries before this, God revealed Himself to a pagan named Abraham. This man was challenged to go into the land of Canaan to become a servant of the most High God. He obeyed and became known as "a friend of God."

His descendants prospered, eventually wresting Canaan from hordes of cruel tribes who had entrenched themselves in the area. The Israelites (as Abraham's descendants were called) lived in the land for a thousand years and were frequently disciplined by God for their attraction to idolatry. Assyria conquered ten regions (or tribes), and later the Babylonians came and conquered the southern part of the land, specifically the city of Jerusalem. They carried off those Israelites to Babylon, but many of them returned to Jerusalem later.

Four hundred years later, Christ was born in Bethlehem, fulfilling the message of judgment God had given to the serpent. And so it was: "But when the fulness of the time came, God sent forth His Son, born of a woman, born under the Law, in order that He might redeem those who were under the Law, that we might receive the adoption as sons" (Galatians 4:4-5).

Christ's primary purpose was to be a sacrifice for sinners, a sacrifice that would be received by God the Father. What that meant was that a part of the human family would not merely alter their allegiance (choosing God rather than Satan), but they would be fully reconciled to God and would receive the coveted status of sons of God.

God defeated Satan's intention to keep all humanity on his side. Of course God could have crushed Satan with raw power, but He chose to do it according to His own laws. He let Satan continue to wield authority over the world, yet He sent Christ to humiliate him by winning a spiritual and moral victory.

Although the death of Christ appeared to be a rather ordinary historical event (indeed, two others were crucified next to Him that very day), it elicited intense, invisible conflict in the spirit world. Satan, though not fully understanding all the implications of what was happening, tried to persuade Christ to avoid the cross and quite possibly sought to kill Him in Gethsemane. But that was just the serpent's attempt to bruise the heel of the woman's seed.

Christ overcame this opposition, of course, and went on to give His blood as a sacrifice for sinners. Satan was crushed. God was reconciling people to Himself, and Satan could do nothing about it. He could only stand by and watch with envy and anger.

This helps us understand Satan's intense desire to see born again believers offend God by committing sins, thereby coming under the sphere of satanic influence. *Anything* to get back at God.

His Greatest Hoax

Christ's sacrifice does not negate Satan's power, however. As an evil being (former angel) he still has all of his attributes intact. He can travel with incredible swiftness from one part of the world to another. He can fight battles with God's angels and organize legions of his underlings into a fearsome army, causing much spiritual destruction. His strength in the spirit world is so awesome that even Michael the archangel, who disputed with him about the body of Moses, treated him with respect (Jude 9).

Yet for all his power, Satan is personally losing ground every single day. The hoax, if it be called such, is his egotistical theory that he is actually able to thwart the purposes and plans of God.

Satan can gloat over the victories he has won: many believers have been defeated in warfare against him. Homes have been wrecked. Christians have backslidden, and unbelievers remain entrenched in sin, because the evil one has snatched the Word of God from their hearts (Mark 4:15). This litany of victories is surely of some delight to the chief destroyer, who has heaped vengeance upon the Almighty.

But all these victories are only a mirage, for they actually further Satan's own destruction. God uses these "defeats" for His own glory. For example, to the casual observer the death of Christ appeared to be a defeat for the Son of God, yet it was truly a defeat for Satan. God will eventually take all of the so-called victories of Satan and turn them upon his own head.

In addition, Satan will be judged for all the evil deeds he commits, and every one of his victories only means his eternal punishment will be that much greater. If he were as wise as he evidently believes he is, he would cease his activity against God immediately!

Don't miss the irony. Satan, whose chief weapon is deception, is evidently himself deceived. Either that, or he, who boasts of his power, lacks even the strength to stop fighting God! He may have physical and spiritual power, but moral power cannot be found in him. Wisdom eludes him.

Nevertheless we must contend with him. He has a plan for us all.

His Greatest Lies

Satan's full-time occupation is to make sin look beneficial to us. He tries to show us the rewards of following our own desires. As already emphasized, he remains hidden, using our natural sinful responses to spring the traps that will keep us bound.

Following are twelve doorways that have this in common: each of them can at some time appear to be an innocent option, yet every one is a deadly trap. They all eventually lead to the same dark room.

REBELLION/SELF-WILL

Because the first sin that was ever committed by Lucifer was rebellion, this sin properly must be listed first. Satan wants us to think that self-will is not abhorrent to God.

Children who rebel against parental authority or adults who refuse to submit to Christ and to church leadership—these and a dozen other kinds of rebellion delight the evil one. The "look out for number one" philosophy did not originate in the human mind but was first embraced by Lucifer when he substituted his will for God's.

Rebellion is like the sin of witchcraft, and insubordination is like idolatry (1 Samuel 15:23). The rebellion of drugs, hard rock music, and violence all play in concert with the devil's tune.

When Paul was listing the qualifications for leadership within the church, he warned that new converts were not ready for such responsibility because of the temptation to pride. He wrote, "and not a new convert, lest he become conceited and fall into the condemnation incurred by the devil" (1 Timothy 3:6).

Our rebellion is as detestable to God as Satan's. To become Satan's servant we need not invite him into our life; we need only to live in rebellion against God and against our properly constituted authorities.

One day a couple decided to sell a piece of property and give some of the proceeds to the church. So far, so good. But they also agreed to pretend that they were contributing all of the money from the sale. Like many of us, they wanted to appear to be better Christians than they really were. The apostle Peter rebuked them and asked the husband, "Ananias, why has Satan filled your heart to lie to the Holy Spirit, and to keep back some of the price of the land?" (Acts 5:3).

Dishonesty in speech and actions is not only consistent with Satan's character, but when we act thus, we play into his hand. To lie is to submit to the authority of the father of lies, the devil.

FEAR

The fear of witnessing for Christ, which all of us tend to experience, seems so natural that we seldom think Satan had anything to do with it. Yet, interestingly, before Peter denied that he knew his Savior, Christ explained, "Simon, Simon, behold, Satan has demanded permission to sift you like wheat; but I have prayed for you, that your faith may not fail; and you, when once you have turned

again, strengthen your brothers"
(Luke 22:31-32).

Fear is one of Satan's most popu-
lar weapons. People are afraid of
crowds, afraid of the future, afraid of
what people will think of them,
afraid to witness, afraid to live. John
wrote, "Fear involves punishment,
and the one who fears is not perfect-
ed in love" (1 John 4:18).

To serve fear is to serve Satan
(Hebrews 2:14-15).

MORAL IMPURITY/ADDICTIONS

There are several reasons sexual
temptations and perversions are often exploited by demonic powers.
One is because of the powerful nature
of sexual attraction and of the desire
for fulfillment. Satan always strikes
where we are weakest. Another reason is that the basic unit of society is
the family, and sexual sin destroys
those relationships.

When Paul was warning the mar-
ried couples in Corinth about the
dangers of prolonged sexual absti-
nence, he encouraged them to "come
together again lest Satan tempt you
because of your lack of self-control"
(1 Corinthians 7:5).

A member of Wycliffe Bible
Translators said that one day while
riding on a plane she noticed that the
couple next to her refused the meal,

32

explaining that they were fasting. She thought that they might be Christians, but they said that they were worshipers of Satan. They were fasting and praying to him that (1) the Billy Graham crusade about to begin in Vancouver would be a failure and (2) Christian ministers would commit adultery so that their witness for Christ would be destroyed.

Satan wants the desires of the flesh to become addictions. People may become governed by alcoholism, drugs, gluttony, or sexual addictions of various kinds. Satan inflames these desires so that they take over a victim's life.

It is not necessary to attend a seance to serve Satan. All you need to do is pursue your particular lustful desires with abandon, letting them take you wherever they may lead. Those who serve lust serve the devil.

COVETEOUSNESS

Coveting the wealth of others may seem to be a harmless occupation. Indeed, our society glories in its unabashed quest for wealth. Some who are millionaires many times over are excruciatingly stingy, hoarding every dime for themselves. According to *Time* magazine, one tycoon whose wealth exceeded $400 million was not known to have given as much as a pair of cuff links to charity.

Why this irrational fascination with more wealth than one could ever use? Paul warned, "For this you know with certainty, that no immoral or impure person or covetous man, who is an idolater, has an inheritance in the kingdom of Christ and God" (Ephesians 5:5).

Covetousness is idolatry, and behind every idol are demonic spirits (1 Corinthians 10:19-20). Satan does not mind which idol we choose, as long as it distracts us from the worship of the true God. Many people who know nothing about Satan have become his most loyal worshipers by becoming consumed with a covetous spirit.

GUILT

The name Adversary means "Accuser."

The prophet Zechariah in one of his visions saw the high priest Joshua (not to be confused with the successor to Moses) standing before the Lord, clothed in filthy garments, which symbolized the sins of the nation. Satan was present too, standing at his right hand to accuse him. But God took the filthy garments from Joshua and clothed him with festal robes (Zechariah 3:1-7).

Whereas the Holy Spirit uses guilt to drive us to Christ for forgiveness, Satan uses guilt to drive a wedge between God and us. He accomplishes this by (1) making us believe that our sins are too great for God to forgive, or (2) making us feel guilty for sins that have already been forgiven.

Satan lies not only with words but with emotions. He attempts to create feelings that alienate us from God, from others, and even from ourselves. He finds it most helpful if we brood in isolation and believe our most painful depressions.

Don't let the irony escape you. Satan incites us to sin, and then if we follow his suggestions, he is the first to heap condemnation upon our conscience. He condemns us for the same sins he entices us to commit!

Thankfully, Satan's work of accusation will finally come to an end: "Now the salvation, and the power, and the kingdom of our God and the authority of His Christ have come, for the accuser of our brethren has been thrown down, who accuses them before our God day and night" (Revelation 12:10).

MURDER/HATRED

We might think that when Cain killed Abel in a fit of jealousy and anger, it was a purely human (though criminal) response to a family feud. But Christ taught that Satan was a murderer from the beginning (John 8:44); therefore we should not think it strange that John wrote that Cain killed his brother because he "was of the evil one" (1 John 3:12).

John affirms that one who does not love his brother is acting like a child of the devil. In contrast, the children of God love one another. And then John adds this startling comment: "Everyone who hates his brother is a murderer; and you know that no murderer has eternal life abiding in him" (1 John 3:15). That explains why some who are controlled by an evil spirit have a persistent desire to commit suicide. Such destruction gives Satan great momentary delight.

He is a murderer and a hater. And those who practice these sins come under his authority.

DOCTRINAL DIVISION

Satan inspires people to veer off into false cults that dethrone Christ. He leads people into strange and preferably occultic doctrines.

"But the Spirit explicitly says that in later times some will fall away from the faith, paying attention to deceitful spirits and doctrines of demons" (1 Timothy 4:1). These doctrines may range from asceticism to doctrines that incite hypocritical rationalizations that lead to a hard heart. (Both are mentioned in this context.)

False cults are too numerous to mention in this booklet. Suffice it to say that many teach that Christ is not fully God or that He is not unique because all of us are gods just as He was. Both heresies mislead multitudes.

There is no need to visit a fortune-teller in order to give your soul to satanic powers. Simply accept false doctrine that obscures the true message of the gospel.

ANGER

One sign of demonic activity is irrational, uncontrollable anger. Fits of temper often erupt with little or no provocation. Paul wrote, "Be angry, and yet do not sin; do not let the sun go down on your anger, and do not give the devil an opportunity" (Ephesians 4:26-27).

The Greek word for "opportunity" is *topos*, which means "a foothold." Anger, like other sins, allows an evil spirit to gain at least partial entry into one's life. That wedge in the door can become the basis for further anger and demonic exploitation.

This is not the place to discuss all of the various bridges that are available to enter the world of the occult. Astrology, Ouija boards, channeling, fortune-telling, Transcendental Meditation, games such as Dungeons and Dragons®—these and dozens of other techniques are practiced today by many who do not know that all such activities belong to the demonic world. Modern notions about exploring the power of the mind and experiencing "the god within us" are based on pagan theologies. The New Age movement is occultism with a friendly American face.

We are also told that the shortcut to a new perception of reality is psychedelic drugs, which bring about a new state of consciousness. These experiences are an open invitation to the demonic world. To seek such mind-expanding techniques is to enter into Satan's kingdom.

MIRACLES

Some individuals experience apparitions or health cures that are actually accomplished through satanic power. We should not be surprised, for the Antichrist will deceive the world with "power and signs and false wonders" (2 Thessalonians 2:9). The infiltration of Eastern mysticism into America has created so-called miraculous cures, visions, and powers, many of which are demonic in nature.

CHILDHOOD TRAUMA

Satan will exploit any negative feelings you may have developed in your past. A child who felt rejected by his parents may actually discover that he is under the influence of a spirit of rejection. There are spirits of anger, bitterness, and revenge. Many people who confront their past suddenly discover that they are controlled (in varying degrees) by spirits that seek to keep them in emotional and spiritual bondage.

Sometimes ancestral spirits remain within the family lineage. One day Christ was asked to cast out a demon from a child who was being thrown to the ground by a wicked spirit and then ground his teeth and stiffened out (Mark 9:18). Christ asked the father how long it had been happening, and he answered, "From childhood" (v. 21). Clearly, that child had committed no sin to invite the spirit. It seems most probable that relatives had been involved in occultic or immoral practices that resulted in a transference of spirits.

These are just some of the doorways Satan uses to gain a degree of control over us. He invites us into his territory by clever deception. We think we are just serving ourselves and do not realize that we are serving him.

HIS GREATEST FEAR

Satan's greatest fear is that Christians will understand that he is defeated and that God has made it possible for us to send him from us. He fears detection and bold confrontation.

One principle that is absolutely essential to realize in our struggle against Satan is that *it is much easier to defend territory that is ours than to reclaim territory that is in the control of the enemy.* A few combat troops can easily defend a hill though they are outnumbered. Once they have entrenched themselves, built reinforcements, and hoarded food and ammunition, they become almost invincible. But once the hill is lost it takes a mighty army to win it back.

Satan's strategy is to get us to surrender some area of our lives to him. His intentions are to (1) make it almost impossible for us to take the territory away from him and to (2) use this stronghold as a launching pad for future conquests.

Have you ever noticed that those who have committed immorality in their past are more easily tempted to fall into the same sin? The same can be said of alcoholism, drug addiction, and gambling. How much better never to have experienced the exhilaration of these sins than to have to root them out once they have become firmly implanted in our lives.

We must learn to recognize Satan's attempts to destroy our witness for Christ by enticing us to submit to his authority.

How do we defend ourselves against satanic attack? And how do we help those who are already bound by him?

THE DEFENSE

1. *We must see all sin as our enemy, never as our friend.* When faced with a moral or spiritual choice, we often think that we can sin without any serious consequences. Sin appears to be our friend. We must remember that if we embrace sin, we embrace the devil. Sin is his playground; it is his trap.

2. *Realize that sometimes the trap does not appear to involve a clear choice between good and evil.* I'm talking about those rationalizations we use when the revealed will of God conflicts with our own emotions or with what seems to be best in our

eyes. A woman may be tempted to marry a divorced man whose divorce had no biblical basis. Worse, a man may marry another woman after divorcing his wife simply on the grounds that his first marriage was not fulfilling. He fails to see the evil in his action because he feels love in his heart for his new partner. The rationalizations are legion.

3. *Realize that you can be trapped by Satan in one single act.* The mouse does not have to have a series of experiences with traps in order to be caught. Just one bite of cheese is sufficient.

Some people resist temptation for many years and yet in one act of weakness make a choice that leads them to ruin. One act of immorality or one foolish choice of a marriage partner— these and other sins have led committed believers into lives of spiritual stagnation and deterioration. Of course God is able to make the best of these situations after repentance and surrender to His will. But He cannot reverse the damage. Just ask King David.

4. *Reject sinful suggestions the moment you become aware of them.* Jesus met Satan saying, "Begone, for it is written. . ." Notice that using Scripture did not cause Satan to flee immediately. He returned with another temptation and then another. Luke writes that Satan finally left,

"waiting for a more opportune time."
Often we must resist Satan just as
Christ did by saying, "Begone, Satan,
for it is written . . . " Then we quote
those promises that assure us of our
victory in Christ.

I've observed that Christians
who do this sometimes give up too
easily. They quote a verse or two, and
if they do not experience immediate
results, they doubt whether God's
Word is effective. But when breaking
a stronghold, we must resist Satan
repeatedly, perhaps for a long period
of time, for he backs off only reluc-
tantly and with the intent to strike
again. For example, a man who wishes
to overcome addiction to pornography should memorize perhaps twenty
verses that can be used at the very
point of temptation.

Be encouraged. *The more often
you successfully resist Satan, the
weaker his temptations will become.*
Eventually, he will simply have to
back off.

5. *Understand that the best defense is the armor of God.* Space for-
bids a detailed explanation of the
armor of God that is available to every Christian. However, this equip-
ment can be put on every day through
prayer. Just read through the pas-
sage in Ephesians that lists each
piece, affirming that you will receive

God's protection for that day (6:13-20).

You may presently be under the influence of a demonic spirit, or perhaps you know someone else who is. I have met people who hear voices that tell them to commit suicide or to kill someone. Sometimes the voices actually speak words of comfort and encouragement.

Others claim to have supernatural experiences or psychic powers. Then there are the addicts—alcoholism, drugs, pornography, and immorality. Some are overcome by strange fears or the desire to blaspheme, tear up the Bible, or break glass in irrational anger. Add to the list those who are chronically depressed.

Where do we begin?

1. *We must understand the gospel.* Christ's death on the cross was a sacrifice for those who believe in Him. His resurrection and ascension completed the work of redemption. Trust in Christ must be personal and singular. Not Christ *and* baptism, or Christ *and* the ordinances. It is never Christ *and*—faith in Christ alone saves.

Without the transforming power of the gospel, no one can be set free from the dominion of darkness and

44

transferred into the kingdom of God's dear Son (Colossians 1:13).

2. *We must understand the complete triumph of Christ over the demonic world.* "When He had disarmed the rulers and authorities, He made a public display of them, having triumphed over them through Him" (Colossians 2:15). We do not fight from the standpoint of weakness or doubt but from the solid rock of victory and faith. Unquestionably, Satan has been crushed. *Now it is our responsibility to exert authority over him.*

3. *We must understand repentance and submission.* To reclaim territory that is occupied by forces of evil, we must confess the sin that Satan is using as a cover. This should involve confession of all occult involvement, specific acts of disobedience, rebellion, and sinful habits and attitudes. If we even anticipate committing the same sins again, Satan may still claim some authority over us. All bridges to our past sins must be demolished.

"Submit therefore to God. Resist the devil and he will flee from you" (James 4:7). There is great power in the name of Christ but only for those who are submissive to His authority. One day the sons of a Jewish priest thought that they could cast out demons in the name of Christ, just as

Paul had done. But one evil spirit answered and said to them, "I recognize Jesus, and I know about Paul, but who are you?" (Acts 19:15). Then the man with the evil spirit leaped upon the two sons and tore off their clothes and sent them away in shame. The name of Christ has tremendous authority but only for those who are under His authority. Submission must precede resistance.

4. *We must understand the power of the Body of Christ.* Not one of us can live the Christian life alone. We are especially vulnerable when we are cut off from the fellowship and prayers of other believers. Some cannot be delivered from satanic bondage without the prayerful guidance and counsel of knowledgable Christians.

Let me recommend the book *The Adversary*, by Mark Bubeck (Moody, 1975), which gives detailed instructions on how to pray effectively against Satan and how to win victories in our lives and the lives of others.

Let us boldly overcome Satan, whom the saints overcame by the blood of the Lamb and the word of their testimony (Revelation 12:11).

Yes, Satan hates us and has a destructive plan for our lives, but we can make sure it is not fulfilled. We can make sure that it will exist only as a dream in his darkened mind. We have the promise, "Greater is He who is in you than he who is in the world" (1 John 4:4).

And again, "But the Lord is faithful, and He will strengthen and protect you from the evil one" (2 Thessalonians 3:3).

You and I can take steps to make sure that Satan's evil plans are shattered. We can know that God loves us, and we can choose *His* plan for our lives.

Books in the Salt and Light series:

Coming to Grips with
    The Antichrist's New Age Roots
    God's Discipline of the Believer
    Heaven
    Hell
    Homosexuality
    The Role of Europe in Prophecy
    Satan's Plan for Your Life
    Unanswered Prayer